Jump and Shout

COMPETITIVE CHEERLEADING

TRACY NELSON MAURER

Rourke
Publishing LLC
Vero Beach, Florida 32964

Project Assistance courtesy of Jennifer Tell, Dance and Cheer Factory, Forest Lake, Minnesota.

The author also extends appreciation to Mike Maurer, Kendall and Lois Nelson, the Rourke team, and the University of Minnesota Alumni Association.

Photo Credits: Cover, pgs 10-bottom, 28, 32, 40, 43, 44 ©PIR
Title, pgs 9-right, 17, 33, 36 ©PHOTOSPORT.COM
pgs 4, 10-top, 20, 23, 30, 34 ©Paul Martinez/PHOTOSPORT.COM
pgs 6, 8, 9-left, 24, 27 ©Peter Schlitt/PHOTOSPORT.COM
pgs 12, 14, 18 ©Getty

Editor: Frank Sloan

Cover and page design: Nicola Stratford

Notice: This book contains information that is true, complete, and accurate to the best of our knowledge. However, the author and Rourke Publishing LLC offer all recommendations and suggestions without any guarantees and disclaim all liability incurred in connection with the use of this information.

Safety first! Activities appearing or described in this publication may be dangerous. Always work with a trained coach and spotters when learning new cheerleading skills.

Library of Congress Cataloging-in-Publication Data

Maurer, Tracy, 1965-
  Competitive cheerleading / Tracy Nelson Maurer.
    p. cm. -- (Jump and shout)
  Summary: "Cheerleaders blend amazing athletic skills and spirited talent to perform breathtaking stunts. They work hard to boost school pride and win over judges at stiff competitions. Coaches expect teamwork, dedication, good grades, and healthy attitudes"--Provided by publisher.
  Includes bibliographical references and index.
  ISBN 1-59515-501-5 (hardcover : alk. paper)
  1. Cheerleading--Juvenile literature. I. Title. II. Series.
LB3635.M29 2006
791.6'4--dc22
                              2005012632

Printed in the USA

cg/cg

Rourke Publishing
1-800-394-7055
www.rourkepublishing.com
sales@rourkepublishing.com
Post Office Box 3328, Vero Beach, FL 32964

TABLE OF CONTENTS

Many people believe that competitive cheerleaders are true athletes.

Chapter 1

SHOWTIME!

Towering speakers pound out dance tunes. Excitement and jittery nerves electrify the air. The crowd cheers wildly. These fans l-o-v-e to cheer for their favorite teams. They openly admit they come just to watch the cheerleaders.

That's O.K. The cheerleaders *are* the show.

Competitive cheerleading teams dazzle audiences with nonstop action set to high-energy music. Every performer constantly moves. While some cheerleaders flip through tumbling runs, others load **stunts**. The group might dance or chant in **unison** before building up to the grand finale—perhaps a **pyramid** that links several stunts together.

Each team's spectacular routine usually lasts just two minutes and thirty seconds. Hundreds of hours of practice whittle down to one brief but all-out performance for the judges.

The Sport Spat

Winning **choreography** blends athletic stunts, smooth dance moves, and powerful tumbling runs with 100% spirit. Positive attitude shines from each smiling, glitter-sprinkled face. Some people call competitive cheerleading an "expressive sport," because it uses body language on top of physical skills to pump up the crowd.

They compare it to competitive gymnastics.

Then again, other people don't think cheerleaders should compete at all. They're also not sure it's a sport. These **purists** see cheerleading's role as strictly supporting sports teams. Cheerleaders should *lead cheers*, they argue. Cheering for yourself doesn't count.

The purists point to a century of cheerleading tradition. From the first cheers led by Johnny Campbell at a University of Minnesota football game in 1889, cheerleaders have encouraged sports teams to Go! Fight! Win!

Along the way, cheerleaders developed a mighty pink and perky **stereotype**. Popularity contests often decided the squads. How they *looked* mattered more than how they *performed*. Beauty overruled brains.

Ah, tradition.

Steeped in Stereotypes

Tradition, stereotypes, and attitudes about female roles limited competitive cheerleading. For decades, Americans generally thought women should stay at home and raise children. If women held jobs, then their work supported men's jobs: Nurses (women) supported doctors (men). Secretaries (women) supported executives (men). See the pattern? You guessed it: Cheerleaders (girls) supported athletes (boys).

In 1972, Congress passed the Title IX Education Amendment. Schools and their sports programs had to provide equal access for both sexes. Girls quickly proved they were just as competitive as boys. Within a year, cheerleaders started cheering for women's sports.

Throughout the 1970s, women strengthened their roles in the workplace. Nurses became doctors. Secretaries became executives. Again, mirroring society, cheerleaders began the shift from supporting a team to competing as a team.

The media noticed. In 1978, CBS broadcast the Collegiate Cheerleading Championships on television. Five years later, ESPN showed the National High School Cheerleading Championship to the world.

Rude and Wrong Stereotype

Boys who cheered battled stereotypes, too. People thought they were sissies. Nobody seemed to remember that boys invented cheerleading and kept it as a boys-only activity for more than 20 years. Today, guys who cheer are stronger and more athletic than ever.

Cable television pumped up competitive cheerleading even more during the "extreme sports" heydays of the 1990s. Flashy routines with risky big-air stunts (without helmets) revealed cheerleading's bold new attitude. Strong, flexible, and daring athletes won cheerleading titles. No sissies here, boy or girl.

Three Cheers

Today, cheerleading breaks into three main areas:

—supporting and cheering for a sports team

—revving up pep rallies, parades, and pre-game and halftime shows

COMPETITIVE CHEER

—performing precise routines to win more points than other cheerleading teams

Can cheerleaders do all three? Absolutely! Sometimes, squads *require* all three. Schools in more than half of the United States sponsor competitive cheerleading squads. Not all of them can afford to sponsor additional sideline spirit squads or performance cheerleaders. So, those schools ask one squad to cover all three areas.

With all that work, why compete? Like most athletes, many cheerleaders simply can't resist the thrill of testing their skills and working to prove they're the best. The pull is so strong that some school squads have totally given up the sidelines for the spotlights.

Chapter 2

UNIVERSAL SPIRIT

Competitive cheerleading's explosive growth in the 1990s helped to feed America's appetite for sports entertainment. Cheer contests on cable television gained viewers, as did other women's athletic events. During that decade, the National Women's Hockey League opened play, and three national women's basketball leagues started, including the Women's National Basketball Association. Cheerleading movies, such as the 2001 hit *Bring It On*, introduced competitive cheerleading to eager audiences.

*Kirsten Dunst and Gabrielle Union starred in the competitive cheerleading movie **Bring It On**.*

Competitive cheerleading in the United States has become one of the fastest-growing athletic activities among girls. Nearly 100,000 school cheerleaders enter contests each year. Add all-star and community cheerleaders from about 2,500 gyms to that number, too.

Across the United States, more and more all-star gyms attract **elite** competitive cheerleaders. All-star teams operate without connections to a certain school. Instead, they hold tough tryouts and invite the best of the best to join their teams. Most all-star gyms charge membership fees.

City teams or community clubs also charge fees and operate without school ties. But unlike all-star squads, they usually welcome different skill levels and cheer for local events as well as enter competitions.

All-star Divisions

All-star competition groups vary depending on the contests and team focus. Some of the common divisions are listed here.

Open
Any number of females and males, in school or graduated, of any age

Large Co-Ed
At least four males and up to 16 females in grades 9 to 12, for a total of 20 athletes on the floor

Small Co-Ed
One to three males and up to 19 females in grades 9 to 12, for a total of 20 athletes on the floor

Super Varsity
From 21 to 30 females in grades 9 to 12

Large Varsity
From 16 to 20 females in grades 9 to 12

Medium Varsity
From 13 to 15 females in grades 9 to 12

Small Varsity
Up to 12 females in grades 9 to 12

Junior Co-Ed / Junior Varsity
All-girl or boy/girl teams in grades 9 and under

Global Growth

An American original, cheerleading has scored international fans around the globe. Overseas U.S. military bases, American football leagues in Europe, cheerleading magazines and videos, and the Internet have helped ignite the competitive cheerleading spirit in about 50 countries.

Most of the world follows U.S. cheerleading standards for technique, judging, and safety. However, other countries typically see cheerleading as a competitive and technical athletic **discipline** similar to gymnastics or martial arts. Since the 1980s, many nations now operate official cheerleading federations to sanction competitions and promote the sport.

Japan has especially caught the cheerleading spirit. Begun in 1988, the Japan Cheerleading Association now serves more than 240,000 people involved with cheerleading activities there.

Japan also hosts the International Cheerleading Federation (ICF). Since 1998, the ICF has provided a central hub for competitive cheerleading's global growth. Member nations participate in the ICF's Cheerleading World Championships. So far, the United States is not a member. The newbie cheer nations compete among themselves.

A Japanese cheer team performance draws a crowd.

Britain's Biggy

Britain hosts one of the oldest "global" contests, the annual British Cheerleading Association (BCA) International Championships. Crowds of thousands cheer for their favorite teams from all over the world. The BCA now includes more than 125 clubs. That's not bad, considering it started with just eight clubs in 1984.

Certainly, the United States ranks as the Big Dog in the cheerleading world. Cheerleading started here. Americans set the standards. But don't get a big head. Stiff competition from the start-up countries pushes the American teams to new heights—literally. Jump for jump, stunt for stunt, the team from Chile almost snatched the crown from the Americans at the 2000 World Cheerleading Championship (not to be confused with the ICF's Cheerleading World Championships, which started a year later).

The National Cheerleaders Association (NCA), one of many "national" groups in the United States, organized that first big nail-biter championship. Since then, the NCA has continued to promote contests and camps around the world.

From Puerto Rico and Colombia to Chile and Malaysia, cheerleaders everywhere want to compete…and win.

Cheerleaders take time to meet their fans.

Olympic Momentum

Cheerleading's international competitions showcase superior athletic talent. And the wow-factor never lets up as more countries participate. Many of the leading contenders, such as the United States, Germany, Britain, and Japan, know Olympic glory from their other sports teams. Some fans think it's possible to see cheerleaders compete for gold medals some day.

A Chinese cheer team pumps up the crowd at a baseball game.

Olympic cheerleading just might be possible. It's also not likely for a long, long time. Bowling, karate, water skiing, and other "major sports" stand ahead of cheerleading, waiting to join the 28 official Summer Olympics sports. So far, 30 sports hold

"recognition" from the International Olympic Committee.

The rules say that the International Olympic Committee must recognize and admit the sport for seven years before the first official medal event. Unfortunately, competitive cheerleading is not recognized—yet.

Olympic planners know cheerleading's appeal. Competitive-style cheerleading teams have put the pizzazz into breaks at Olympic basketball games. In 2004, a bikini-clad team from Spain's Canary Islands shook up the downtimes at the Olympics' beach volleyball games.

Another advantage? Like many other Olympic sports, competitive cheerleading uses a universal language. Smiles translate perfectly.

Cheery Fact

Experts estimate 4 million cheerleaders show their spirit in about 50 countries.

*Competitive cheerleading may some day
be an Olympic event.*

Chapter 3

THE CONTESTS

Cheerleading competitions and camps continue to grow across the United States. Some 50 organizations and businesses cater to cheerleaders. College, high school, and youth teams choose from more than 70 national and regional events each year. Rival organizations, such as the National Cheerleaders Association and the Universal Cheerleading Association, sanction the largest contests.

Hundreds of teams send videos to earn a chance to compete at national events. About 180 teams, including some dance teams, might make the cut. Less experienced teams look for local contests to build their skills before tackling the big leagues.

Texas claims to be the Cheerleading State, but Florida has become the top spot for contests. Both Walt Disney World in Orlando and Daytona Beach host major cheerleading, baton twirling, and dance competitions. Cheerleaders flock to events on cruise ships and in shopping malls, too. You can catch national contests on national and cable broadcasts.

Rewarding Events

Every contest is run slightly differently than the others. A few **invitationals** select only elite or specialty teams. You must receive an invitation to compete. However, most contests allow any team to qualify by sending a video and an application.

Entry divisions, rules, and judging systems vary. Always read the descriptions carefully, even if your coach picks the contests. Know what to expect.

Popular Contests

In 1988, only 8 regional or national cheer contests existed. Now there are more than 70!

Cheerleading competitions draw teams from all over the country.

Warm-weather states host many national contests.

Entry fees range from a few dollars per cheerleader to about $100 each—no travel, hotel, food, or other costs included. Often, teams raise money with car washes, goodie sales, and special events to help cover the expenses.

The rewards for winning change from year to year, and from event to event, too. At some contests, all competitors receive a trophy or a T-shirt for participating. Other competitions hand out trophies only to the top finishers. Winners might take home medals, gift certificates, clothing, and other prizes. Cheerleading companies might give away items to encourage you to buy their products, too.

Safety Always Wins

College teams build stunts with bases holding a middle stunt level that launches a flyer, the top-level cheerleader, up into the air. They stand almost two stories high, and no one wears a helmet.

The Largest-ever Title

Competitions usually allow no more than 30 cheerleaders on stage at one time. To win the official World Record for the largest-ever cheerleading routine, 435 cheerleaders in matching uniforms from the Cov Squad (Coventry) and Bedworth Babes performed a six-minute routine in unison on July 4, 2004, in Bedworth, United Kingdom.

Not surprisingly, high school teams must keep their stunts to two-people high. They don't wear helmets, either.

Fortunately, head injuries happen very rarely. Spotters, the team members or coaches watching for falling flyers, do a better job than ever. Special spotter training and lots of practice help prevent nasty crashes. Head injuries from cheerleading have, however, caused **paralysis** and death.

Most injuries in competitive cheerleading involve ankles, knees, and wrists. Even during competitions, cheerleaders wear braces or wrap tender spots. Still, cheerleaders report fewer injuries than other school athletes do.

Overall, research shows that cheerleading is a relatively safe activity—provided cheerleaders use safety mats and practice with a trained supervisor.

The National Council for Spirit Safety and Education and the American Association of Cheerleading Coaches and Advisors are among the leading groups dedicated to keeping cheerleading safe. Training camps, safety courses, and certificate programs teach coaches the safest ways for their teams to learn and practice cheers.

Thankfully, most cheerleading injuries are minor.

Safety Check

You, your parents, your coach, and your school or gym share responsibility for safety. Check out your coach's experience, the practice facilities, and all the rules. Tell your parents to ask for better safety measures, if you think they're needed. Mind the safety rules, too. Cheerleading stunts come with enough risks. Don't add to them.

Head and neck injuries are treated very carefully.

Your squad should have:

- [ ] A knowledgeable coach and trainer(s) with safety, first aid, and CPR certification

- [ ] Roomy practice facilities with high ceilings

- [ ] Proper equipment, such as harnesses for jump training and thick floor mats

- [ ] Regular warm-up routines and stretching exercises before every practice and performance

- [ ] Regular cool-down routines and stretching exercises after every practice and performance

- [ ] Spotter training and practice sessions

- [ ] Safety talks about school policies and emergency plans

- [ ] Rules that require an annual medical examination and your parents' approval

- [ ] Rules that ban jewelry and gum during practices and performances; smoking, drinking, and drugs should be banned 24/7, all year long

Competitive cheerleaders work with spotters for safety.

As long as you run, climb, jump, and flip as a cheerleader, then you risk injury. Lower the risk by staying focused and following the rules. Ask questions, if you're not sure about a move. Always use a spotter when you try a new stunt. And don't try stunts above your ability level.

Common sense makes safety sense.

Chapter 4

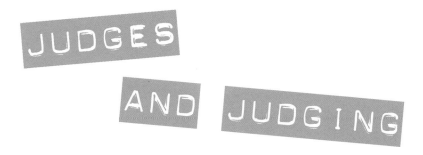

JUDGES AND JUDGING

Cheering in front of your school's fans takes guts. Cheering for just a few judges—that takes steel nerves.

If you're ready for competition, expect to practice every day. Some teams practice three hours a day, Monday through Friday. Sometimes they add in a few weekend practices before a big competition.

Many cheerleading squads put in more practice time than their school basketball or football teams do. On the college level, National Collegiate Athletic Association (NCAA) rules limit sports team practices to 20 hours a week. Cheerleaders might clock 25 hours in a week. But NCAA rules don't apply to cheerleading. According to the NCAA, it's not a sport.

Score, Score, Score Those Points

   Every contest sets its own rules and uses unique score sheets. Take time to study the rules. Most contests use a system with 100 possible points to help keep the judging fair.

A good team spends countless hours training.

For example, the Universal Cheerleaders Association judging sheet sets aside up to 35 points for crowd leading, 45 points for skills, and another 20 points for overall presentation. Some parts of each section carry more weight than others.

Depending on the contest, judges might score all areas or they might divide duties. Each judge then scores certain sections, such as stunt skills or

Judges look for well-rounded teams.

tumbling moves. Some contests assign a **penalty** judge to check that teams follow the rules.

Judges make **subjective** decisions. Your brilliant stunt might leave one judge breathless and leave another one yawning. You just never know.

Contest organizers try to bring together judges with technical knowledge and contest experience. Some associations offer judge training and certification programs. Good judging improves the contest for everyone. Even if you don't win, you can learn what to do better next time.

What Judges Watch

Study the contest's judging form, which is usually available well in advance. Practice your weakest areas over and over again. Mistakes at practice make good lessons for the real show.

Cheerleading Skills

Sharp motions, strong jumps, fluid tumbling, and well-formed stunts attract attention. Judges notice if you're nailing difficult moves.

Projection

Clear and loud voices, direct eye contact, and positive body language say a lot to the judges about the team's confidence and **poise**.

Showmanship

Smooth, crowd-pleasing choreography with unison movements wins over judges. Bold visual effects from **synchronized** motions, props such as **pompons**, or dance steps can add points, too.

Exciting showmanship earns points from the judges.

Team Spirit

Have fun! Crowds respond to happy faces. Smile through the jitters and the butterflies bashing around in your stomach. Show your sportsmanship before, during, and after your performance.

When the judges announce the winners, they could burst your bubble. Disappointment hurts. Hold back your tears. Congratulate the winning team.

Do your best when you perform. Then you can walk out the door with pride and honor—even if it's without a trophy.

Graceful Goofs

Stay focused. If you hit a glitch or goof up a move, handle it gracefully. No stopping, giggling, swearing, or crying.

Chapter 5

WINNING ROUTINES

One strong decision maker guides every competitive cheerleading team. Usually, the coach makes the tough calls. At tryouts, the coach shapes the team by selecting promising cheerleaders who fit the team's style. It's not easy to turn away anyone.

During practice, the coach directs the warm-ups, drills, and routines—always putting safety first. The team learns new stunts through **progression training**. You master one part of the stunt before adding another part.

The coach checks that everyone sticks to the rules. You must show up on time for every practice. Study hard for good grades in school. Don't smoke. Don't drink. Don't do drugs. Rule breakers won't catch a break.

Behind the scenes, the coach decides which contests to enter and what kinds of routines to develop. Many coaches create their own choreography. Sometimes the school or gym hires a professional choreographer to showcase the team's strengths. The coach orders any uniforms or props and arranges for a professional studio to record the routine's music. The coach also assigns the bases, flyers, and spotters.

Whew. And that's not juggling fund-raisers, travel arrangements, or the actual show-day duties.

Keep The Code

Many Coaches ask everyone, including parents, to sign a Code of Conduct pledge. More than a squad rulebook, the Code explains how everyone should behave. The Code covers practices and performances, and your life 24/7 for 12 months. Here's a sample you can use for your team.

OFFICIAL TEAM CODE OF CONDUCT PROMISE

1. _____*(your name here)*_____, an important member of the _____*(your squad's name here)* team, agree to follow this Code of Conduct:

Sportsmanship

1. I will respect my mind and my body. I will seek healthy experiences that promote my growth in a positive way.
2. I will show respect and good sportsmanship to others at all times and expect the same from my team members.
3. I understand that I am a role model and I will represent my team, school, and community well.

Teamwork

1. I will maintain a C average or higher in my academic studies, and I will help my team members do the same.
2. I will not arrive late more than twice or miss more than two practices in one month.
3. I will not wear my uniform for any reason except official performances.

Safety Rules

1. I accept that competitive cheerleading poses risks and that I am responsible for putting safety first.
2. I will follow the team rules, school rules, parent rules, and contest rules, including all safety and performance guidelines both by the spirit and the letter of the rule.
3. I will accept the coach and judge rulings as final.

Cheerleader signature:_____

Parent signature:_____

Coach signature:_____

Date:_____

Details, Details, Details

Some coaches call it all. Others ask assistant coaches, parents, or managers to help. Managers might be former cheerleaders, trainers, or students interested in cheerleading but not on the team. Coaches often assign a team captain or co-captains to assist with the day-to-day and showtime details, too.

You might not like every decision. Unless the team's safety is at stake, think a while before you say anything. Nobody likes gripers or whiners. Disagree respectfully, if you must. Back your opinion with good reasons that help the entire team—not just you. Make positive suggestions. Then politely accept the coach's final decision.

The Four Ps

Competitive cheerleading takes the Four Ps:
* Practice
* Patience
* Perseverance
* Positive attitude

Helping Hands

Coaches need more hours in a day and more hands to do it all. You can give the coach more time by volunteering to handle some tasks. Maybe you can make photocopies or fill water bottles. Offer to schlep gear, set up equipment, or run for forgotten stuff.

Study up. Use the library and Internet to check out the contest organization and facilities ahead of time. Scout the host location for cheerleading suppliers (in case something breaks), restaurants, film developers, or any other businesses you might need.

Make checklists of everything each cheerleader must bring to the competition. Distribute the checklists a week before the event. E-mail a reminder to each team member with a special Go-Team note on the day before you leave. Include a schedule showing where everyone needs to go and when.

Ask a parent or another adult to take notes or pictures during your performance. Share the photos with the team later. Review the notes and talk about how you could improve.

Most important, have fun!

Team players always make an effort to pitch in.

Competitive cheerleading can be a rewarding experience.

Further Reading

Cheerleading in Action by John Crossingham.
　　Crabtree Publishing Company, New York, New York, 2003.

Let's Go Team: Cheer, Dance, March / Competitive Cheerleading
　　by Craig Peters. Mason Crest Publishers, Philadelphia, 2003.

The Ultimate Guide to Cheerleading
　　by Leslie Wilson. Three Rivers Press, New York, New York, 2003.

Web Sites

American Association of Cheerleading Coaches and Advisors
http://www.aacca.org/

British Cheerleading Association
www.cheerleading.org.uk

CheerHome.com, an online information clearinghouse
http://www.CheerHome.com/

Collegiate Cheerleading Company
http://www.collegiatecheerleading.com

Guinness World Records
http://www.guinnessworldrecords.com

Japan Cheerleading Association
http://www.jca-hdqrs.org

Ms. Pineapple's Cheer Page
http://www.mspineapple.com/

National Cheerleaders Association
http://www.nationalspirit.com/

National Council for Spirit Safety & Education
http://www.spiritsafety.com/

National Federation of State High School Associations
http://www.nfhs.org

Glossary

choreography (KOR ee OG ruh fee) — the plan or patterns for dance steps, movement, or action, usually set to music

discipline (DIS uh plin) — an area or subject of special training, study, or practice

elite (uh LEET) — the best or top choice from a group

invitationals (IN vuh TAY shuh nulz) — competitions limited to only those who have been invited

paralysis (puh RAL uh sus) — loss of movement

penalty (PEN ul tee) — punishment or loss assigned because of a broken rule; a penalty judge watches for broken rules

poise (POYZ) — grace, self-confidence, unruffled presence

pompon (POM pon) — in cheerleading, the tufted accessory used to add movement, color, and sound to performances; some dictionaries also use pompom or pom-pom

progression training (pruh GRESH un TRAYN ing) — a method of building skills based on mastering one part before adding the next part

purists (PYOOR usts) — people with strictly held ideas about something

pyramid (PIR uh MID) — in cheerleading, several stunts connected by the top-level, or flyer

stereotype (STAIR ee oh TYP) — right or wrong, a commonly believed and simple image or idea about a group of people

stunts (STUNTZ) — in cheerleading, the poses, jumps, or other tricky moves that accent a cheer

subjective (sub JEK tiv) — a personal opinion based more on emotions, experience, or mood than objective fact

synchronized (SIN kruh NYZD) — performed at the same rate and exactly together

unison (YOO nuh sun) — something done the same way at the same time

Index

About The Author

Tracy Nelson Maurer specializes in nonfiction and business writing. Her most recently published children's books include the *Roaring Rides* series, also from Rourke Publishing LLC. Tracy lives near Minneapolis, Minnesota with her husband Mike and their two children.